A Tsunami Unfolds

Written by Susan Korman
and Kimiko Kajikawa

Acknowledgments
The publisher would like to thank the following for their kind permission to reproduce their photographs: (Key: b-bottom; c-center; l-left; r-right; t-top) **Alamy Images:** Aflo Co., Ltd. 23t, 26r, David L. Moore - JP 22-23b, Eirepix 14, epa european pressphoto agency b.v. 20, 21b, 28t, Henry Westheim Photography 30, Hideo Kurihara 25b, Jeremy sutton-hibbert 29, 31t, Jim West 10r, JTB MEDIA CREATION, Inc. 11, Mark Pearson 15t, MPAK 24, NG Images 13, Pavel Chernobrivets 6b, Pictura Collectus 19t, 19c, Robert Gilhooly 26l, 28b, The Natural History Museum 9, WENN UK 15b, 19b, ZUMA Press, Inc. 5, 17; **Getty Images:** JIJI PRESS / AFP 18, Kurita KAKU / Gamma-Rapho via 10l, MIKE CLARKE / AFP 22bl, Sankei 25t, TOSHIFUMI KITAMURA / AFP 27; **Shutterstock.com:** AISA - Everett 21t, Cico 4, matin 7t, 9t, 11c, 15c, 18b, 23c, 25c, 31bc, Mopic 12, Robyn Mackenzie 6c, 22c, 27t, 28c, 30c; **Yumi Otomo:** Yumi Otomo 7cr, 31

Cover images: Front: **Alamy Images:** Eirepix; Back: **Alamy Images:** Eirepix; **Getty Images:** JIJI PRESS / AFP

All other images © Pearson Education **Picture Research by:** Caitlin Swain

Every effort has been made to trace the copyright holders and we apologize in advance for any unintentional omissions. We would be pleased to insert the appropriate acknowledgment in any subsequent edition of this publication.

With very special thanks to Yumi Otomo for allowing us to publish her personal experience of the 2011 Tsunami in this book.

PEARSON

ISBN-13: 978-0-328-83296-5
ISBN-10: 0-328-83296-0

2 3 4 5 6 7 8 9 10 V0B4 19 18 17 16 15

Contents

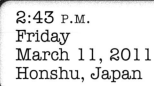
An Unexpected Emergency

It was an ordinary Friday afternoon. Children were at school, and parents were working or taking care of young children at home. Out on the Pacific Ocean, fishermen were hauling in their nets. In busy cities in Japan, such as Tokyo and Sendai, restaurants, shops, and subways were bustling as usual.

Two days earlier a strong earthquake had hit the Tohoku region, but it hadn't caused any damage. Suddenly, seismographs began recording powerful new vibrations—it was another earthquake!

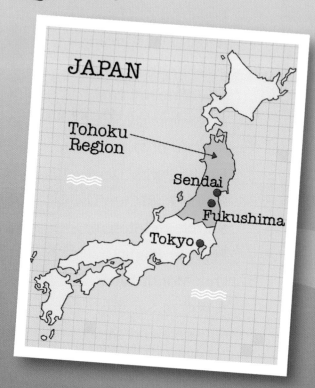

JAPAN

Tohoku Region

Sendai

Fukushima

Tokyo

Seismographs measure the strength of earthquakes.

The quake's epicenter was in the water, about eighty miles from the city of Sendai in the Tohoku region. The Japanese early-warning system quickly sent out alerts.

Emergency Earthquake Alert.
Expect vibrations to begin soon.

People ran to find safe places. High-speed trains, gas lines, power plants, and factories automatically shut down.

The quake hit at 2:46 P.M. The ground rumbled and a loud roar filled the air. Ceilings split, roofs caved in, bookshelves and objects crashed to the floor. Tall skyscrapers swayed, and roads cracked and buckled.

Did You Know?

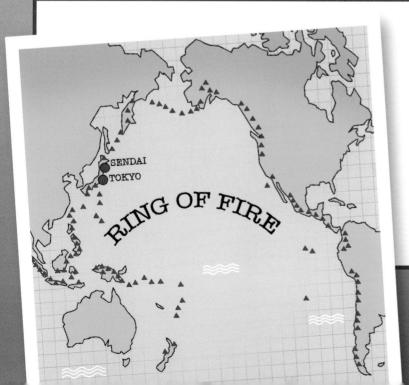

SENDAI
TOKYO
RING OF FIRE

The Ring of Fire

The Japanese islands are located in the Ring of Fire. About ninety percent of the world's earthquakes occur in this region. It contains a string of active volcanoes, and several tectonic plates meet here.

Japan's Biggest Earthquake

Earthquakes are common in Japan. However, the people instantly knew that something was different about this quake.

They were right; this earthquake was a big one, measuring 9.0 on the Richter scale of magnitude. This was one of the strongest quakes in history. It went on for six long minutes. The earthquake was so powerful that it moved Japan's main island, Honshu, about eight feet to the east!

MONSTER 9.0 EARTHQUAKE STRONGEST EVER RECORDED IN JAPAN

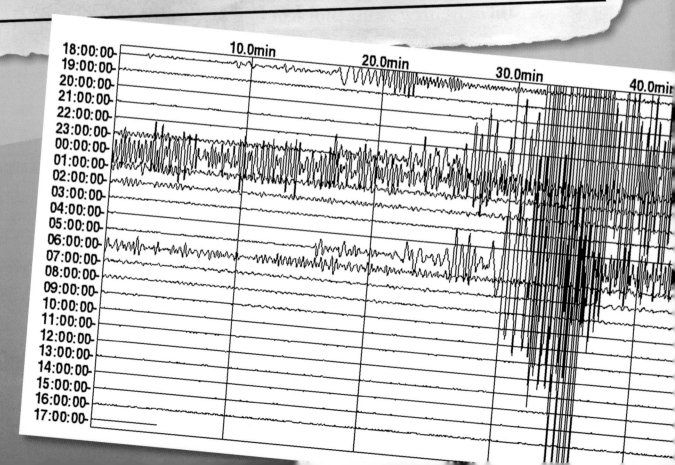

Yumi's Experience

Yumi, a Japanese woman, was working as a security officer at Sendai Airport on March 11, 2011. The airport is located about one mile from the coast.

That morning, Yumi drove to work as usual and parked her car in a parking lot. When the earthquake struck the airport, many people were confused and frightened. Yumi was stunned by how strong it was and how long it lasted. The powerful vibrations shook the building hard and collapsed the ceiling inside the airport's central hall.

50.0min

Did You Know?

The Richter Scale

The Richter scale is the most common scale used for measuring an earthquake's strength or magnitude. It is named after Charles F. Richter, an American seismologist who developed it in 1935.

Powerful Aftershocks

After the main shock of the earthquake, powerful aftershocks kept coming. Most buildings held up well, but the worst damage was along the coast. The quake had damaged thousands of homes. It also damaged Sendai airport, and ripped pipes and lockers from walls at the Daiichi Nuclear Power Plant in Fukushima.

Did You Know?

Taking Time

The earthquake was felt as far away as China, Taiwan, and Russia. It not only moved the island of Honshu, but was so powerful that it also sped up Earth's rotation on its axis. That made each day shorter by 1.8 microseconds!

The World's Biggest Earthquakes

The Japan 2011 earthquake was the fourth most powerful ever recorded.

WHERE?	WHEN?	HOW BIG?
Southern Chile	1960	9.5 magnitude
Prince William Sound, Alaska, U.S.A	1964	9.2 magnitude
Northern Sumatra, Indonesia	2004	9.1 magnitude
Northern Japan	2011	9.0 magnitude
Kamchatka, Russia	1952	9.0 magnitude

The quake had knocked out electricity in many parts of Japan. With millions of people trying to use their phones, phone networks were crashing too. Most people living in Japan assumed that the worst part of the disaster was over. But for millions—especially those living close to the epicenter—the disaster was just beginning.

Did You Know?

Messenger from the Sea

In Japan, the oarfish is known as the "messenger from the sea god's palace." Some people believe that the rare appearance of these fish on beaches is a signal that an earthquake is about to strike. Before the quake in 2011, about twenty oarfish were seen stranded on beaches.

A Tsunami Warning

About nine minutes after the earthquake hit, regional alarms sounded again. A tsunami was coming, and it was coming fast.

Did You Know?

What Is a Tsunami?

A tsunami is a series of waves in the ocean created by earthquakes or by volcanic eruptions or landslides. The waves of a tsunami can travel as fast as a jet plane—500 miles per hour!

Along the coast, people were used to getting tsunami alerts after earthquakes. In fact, when it came to tsunami preparation, many experts considered Japan's to be the best in the world. Children practiced safety drills in school. Warning signs with evacuation routes were posted along the coastline. Large sea walls stood along the sea, built to hold back tall waves.

TSUNAMI HAZARD ZONE

IN CASE OF EARTHQUAKE, GO TO HIGH GROUND OR INLAND

Shindo

In Japan, a seismic intensity scale is used to measure an earthquake's strength. The intensity is recorded in units called shindo, which means "degree of shaking."

Real Life

Yumi's Experience

At the airport, Yumi heard the tsunami alarm ringing after the quake. Soon many local residents arrived, seeking shelter. The nearby area was flat and easily flooded, and the airport was one of the tallest structures around.

Many locals were elderly people. Airport employees and others began assisting them to get to the airport's higher floors.

Sendai Airport before the 2011 tsunami.

Scrambling for Safety

By now, the sky above the coast was dark. The sea was churning. Loudspeaker systems were blaring warnings again and again: *Save yourselves! Immediately evacuate to higher ground! Save yourselves!*

Did You Know?

How a Tsunami Forms

An earthquake is caused by the sudden movement of Earth's tectonic plates. This violent movement displaces huge amounts of water, which creates waves in the sea. As the waves travel toward land, they grow larger and can become deadly.

This image shows the outline of Earth's tectonic plates.

Did You Know?

Sea Walls

Japan has used sea walls to protect villages from the sea for many years. Sea walls can make people think they are safe, and stop them from evacuating. But the sea walls can't always protect people against the giant waves of a tsunami.

Parents rushed to locate their children. Inside buildings, people hurried to roofs and higher floors. Outdoors, people ran toward high ground. Some fishermen raced to the water, scrambling to get their boats out of the water before the tsunami hit.

Meanwhile, people with electricity or Internet access were checking TVs and computers to get the latest news. The news was terrifying. Satellites high above Earth had captured images of the tsunami. It was absolutely massive.

The Tsunami Hits

The first wave hit the coast about fifteen to thirty minutes after the tsunami warnings came. From a distance, people could see a huge black shape rising into the air. At first, it looked like smoke or a cloud. Then people realized the black plume was actually the tsunami crashing into the shore!

Did You Know?

Harbor Wave

A tsunami is also called a tidal wave or a seismic wave. In Japanese, the word *tsunami* is represented by two characters: *tsu* meaning "harbor" and *nami* meaning "wave."

津波
tsunami

The enormous waves—128 feet in some areas—sailed right over the sea walls. Then the water smashed onto land, picking up everything in its path: cars, houses, boats, buildings, pets, and people. It rolled through villages and streets, turning darker and darker as it swept up more debris.

Real Life

Yumi's Experience

Only about twenty minutes passed before the water arrived from the east. It was carrying everything with it—homes, hundreds of cars, and many, many people. Of course, people on land were trying to flee by car. But the water was much faster. It surrounded the airport in minutes.

A Nuclear Disaster?

At the Daiichi power plant, located on Japan's northeast coast, another crisis was brewing. The plant's nuclear reactors had shut down automatically after the earthquake alerts, and now back-up generators were on. The generators were doing a critical job: keeping the reactors' cores cool to prevent a nuclear meltdown.

Did You Know?

Nuclear Power in Japan

In 2011, Japan had fifty-four nuclear reactors that produced about thirty percent of the country's electricity. The Daiichi plant, known as "Number One," had six of these reactors.

Workers were busy monitoring damage from the quake when the giant tsunami surprised them, crashing right over the plant's sea wall. Water poured into the lower floors, flooding the plant's generators. Workers quickly grew alarmed—if the generators stopped working, it would become a very dangerous situation.

3.25 p.m. March 11, 2011
#Quake hit Daiichi plant hard. checking damage now.

Did You Know?

What Is a Nuclear Meltdown?

The core of a nuclear reactor gets very hot. In order to prevent overheating, a cooling system keeps the core cool. If this cooling system fails, the fuel rods inside the reactor can begin to melt and release dangerous levels of radiation into the air and water.

17

A Wave of Destruction

Many people took photos of the incredible tsunami as it swept across northeast Japan. People from all over the world watched too, as TV stations and the Internet broadcast live images.

LIVE

BREAKING NEWS

DEADLY WAVES HIT COAST

Real Life

Rikuzentakata, Japan

Setsuko, a cook at a nursery school, ignored the tsunami warning at first. Similar warnings came all the time, and the school was a mile from the sea; tsunamis never traveled this far inland. But minutes after the earthquake, a mysterious dark shape in the distance caught her eye—the tsunami! It was rushing toward the school! The powerful water could destroy the wooden school building in minutes. Setsuko and the teachers quickly gathered all of the children and raced toward a nearby hill, getting them to safety.

The water swept across land, and then it began rolling back toward the sea, carrying more debris with it. At Sendai airport, it dumped hundreds of cars, trucks, and even planes.

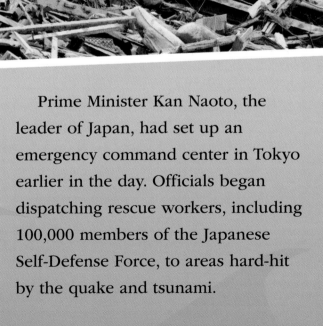

Prime Minister Kan Naoto, the leader of Japan, had set up an emergency command center in Tokyo earlier in the day. Officials began dispatching rescue workers, including 100,000 members of the Japanese Self-Defense Force, to areas hard-hit by the quake and tsunami.

19

Dealing with Destruction

That night, temperatures dropped, and it was snowing in some areas. People huddled together in dark evacuation centers while strong aftershocks kept rumbling.

Across the country about six million homes were without electricity, and one million were without water. Many people had no food or heat.

7.30 p.m. March II, 2011
#Quake High school flooded but students are safe on third floor.

Did You Know?

The Wave That Traveled Around the World

In Hawaii, the tsunami created waves eleven to twelve feet high. Nine-foot-high waves reached California and Oregon in the United States, sinking boats and destroying a harbor. About eighteen hours after the quake, waves from the tsunami reached the coast of Antarctica, where they cracked the ice shelf.

Worst of all, many people were separated from their families with no way to find out who had survived and who had died. Roads were blocked and the train service was shut down. Many people, especially in cities such as Tokyo and Sendai, started walking home. In some cases, the long trek would take days.

Did You Know?

Thucydides

Thucydides was a historian from ancient Greece. He was the first to record a connection between earthquakes and tsunamis. He wrote that the first sign of a tsunami is often the sudden draining of a harbor as the sea pulls away from the coast.

21

Rising Radiation Levels

At the Daiichi plant, workers struggled to manage the nuclear crisis. The floodwaters had damaged the generators, so crews were desperately pumping sea water into the reactors to keep them cool. By now, radiation levels near the plant measured eight times higher than normal. Officials ordered thousands of people living near the plants to evacuate.

GOVERNMENT DECLARES STATE OF EMERGENCY AT "NUMBER ONE"

Did You Know?

The World Helps

Many countries prepared to send search-and-rescue teams to Japan. Other nations and relief organizations promised supplies and money. Individuals and private organizations, such as schools and churches, helped by organizing volunteers and donating supplies.

Real Life

Yumi's Experience

Hundreds of people were still trapped inside the airport. Water surrounded the buildings and cars, trucks, and planes had been tossed everywhere. A fire had started in one section of the airport.

Yumi recalls that the people at the airport tried to stay calm. Everyone kept helping one another, rationing food and drinks that came from shops and vending machines inside the airport. People controlled themselves, taking very little food or drink. They had no idea how long they would be stranded there, so they were careful to make all their supplies last.

Search and Rescue

Military helicopters had been flying over the disaster zone to assess the damage. Slowly, long lines of trucks reached hard-hit areas. The rescuers' work was difficult—and often heart-breaking.

Nearly ten thousand people were missing in the town of Minamisanriku. Six hundred people were trapped on the roof of an elementary school in Sendai. Doctors and nurses were waving pink umbrellas to attract rescuers' attention at a hospital in Iwanuma.

5.15 p.m. March 12, 2011
#Quake damage much worse than imagined. Tears in our eyes when we arrived.

While most of the work involved recovering those who had been killed, emergency workers rescued many people too. Using specially-trained dogs, they carefully searched for victims in the rubble.

Real Life

Yumi's Experience

After three days, Yumi was finally able to leave the airport. Her car had been carried off by the tsunami, so she, like many others, walked home.

Yumi was thrilled to see that her family was fine, and her home was still standing. But water had destroyed nearly all of her neighborhood. Many neighbors had lost everything. Several people moved in with Yumi's family. For a long time, they had no gas, water, or electricity.

Fight or Flight?

People in shelters found ways to survive by building fires and locating supplies in nearby buildings. Thousands desperately searched for missing loved ones, posting notices in public spaces.

Around the world, people were amazed by the patience of Japanese victims. They waited in long lines for food and other supplies.

In Fukushima, officials reported more grim news. Two of the reactors had experienced hydrogen explosions, and partial meltdowns had occurred. The evacuation zone around Daiichi was being expanded. Officials had begun scanning people and pets with radiation detectors to check radiation levels.

DAIICHI NUCLEAR DISASTER WORST IN HISTORY?

Government officials frequently updated the people. But many Japanese citizens mistrusted these reports. They suspected that radiation levels were actually much higher, and they worried about contamination of food supplies. A huge number of people fled the area.

Did You Know?

Amazing Rescues

- Two days after the disaster, a man in his sixties was found alive at sea, still clinging to the roof of his house.

- A family's home was completely flooded, but their dogs were found upstairs, still alive.

- All eighty-one passengers aboard a boat were safely airlifted after being tossed around in a whirlpool from the tsunami.

One Month Later . . .

One month after the tsunami, people across Japan created memorials and stood in silence to remember victims. Many threw flowers into the sea.

JAPAN STILL FACING MANY CHALLENGES

By now, some people had returned to work and school, but most had not yet returned to any kind of normal life. Thousands were still in temporary housing.

The situation at Daiichi remained a nuclear emergency. Radiation levels there were so high that workers were using robots to assess damage. The government had shut down Japan's fifty remaining nuclear plants for inspection.

The earthquake and tsunami in Japan were the most recorded disasters in history. This means that scientists had a lot of new data to study, which could lead to valuable new lessons about earthquakes and tsunamis.

Government officials were also studying the disasters. What had gone wrong on March 11, 2011? How could Japan—a well-prepared nation— avoid such massive damage in the future?

Did You Know?

Illnesses from the Tsunami

Many people developed health problems such as "tsunami lung," a lung disease caused by exposure to contaminated water. Hypothermia was another common problem. People also worried that exposure to radiation would cause future illnesses.

A Will to Survive

Japan created new tsunami evacuation plans and taller sea walls.

New sensors helped to predict disasters more accurately and improve warning systems. The rebuilding of homes continued. But for many, its pace was slow and frustrating.

TWO YEARS LATER, 300,000 STILL IN TEMPORARY HOUSING

Most Fukushima residents decided never to return to the contaminated area. When two nuclear reactors were restarted in Japan, thousands protested. Other countries began rethinking the use of nuclear power too.

Did You Know?

Damage from March 11, 2011

The disasters killed about nineteen thousand people. The estimated cost of the damage was about $210 billion.

For a long while, the people of Japan were in shock. Many doubted the government's ability to rebuild and protect Japan. But during the crisis, people helped one another and discovered their own inner strength. That gave them hope and a strong will to survive.

March 11, 2012
#Quake crowd gathered at sea today to remember.

Real Life

Yumi's Experience

Yumi remembers the terrible destruction in 2011. Yet she also remembers something else—people's amazing response. She saw no one trying to take advantage of others, even when his or her own survival was at stake. Instead, she witnessed people doing their best to support each other. It was this kind of support that helped Yumi heal and recover.

31

Glossary

aftershock	smaller earthquake that happens after a previous large earthquake, in the same area as the main shock
contamination	effect of dirt, chemicals or radiation that make something harmful
debris	items left after something has been destroyed
epicenter	center of an earthquake
evacuation	move from somewhere dangerous to a place of safety
hypothermia	condition where someone is very ill because their body has been extremely cold for a long time
magnitude	size and strength of an earthquake
nuclear reactor	machine used at nuclear power plants to make electricity
radiation	harmful particles given out by radioactive substances
relief organization	organizations that provide help to people
seismograph	instrument that measures the strength of an earthquake
seismologist	scientist who studies earthquakes
tectonic plate	one of a series of giant pieces of rock that make up Earth's surface, whose movement can cause earthquakes

Index